WEIGHT GAIN

COOKBOOK

For Seniors

Nutritious Recipes And Expert Tips To Increase Calorie Intake And Enhance Overall Health

LEONA BUTLER

TABLE OF CONTENT

Chapter 3

Delectable Lunch Recipes To Put On Weight

1. CHICKEN AND QUINOA SALAD
2. SWEET POTATO AND BLACK BEAN BOWL:
3. SALMON AND VEGETABLE STIR-FRY
4. MUSHROOM AND SPINACH OMELETTE:
5. PASTA PRIMAVERA WITH GRILLED CHICKEN:
6. TURKEY AND VEGGIE WRAP:
7. BEAN AND LENTIL SOUP:
8. BAKED COD WITH ROASTED VEGETABLES
9. GREEK YOGURT PARFAIT
10. FISH AND RICE BOWL

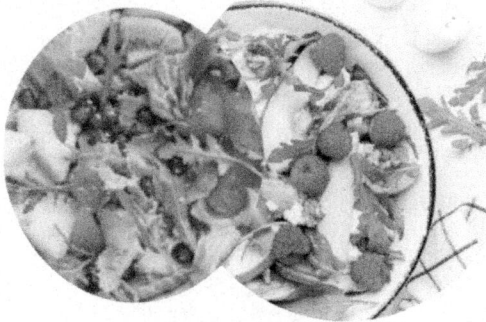

Chapter 4
Satisfying Dinners Recipes

1. CREAMY CHICKEN ALFREDO PASTA:
2. QUINOA AND BLACK BEAN BOWL:
3. SALMON AND SWEET POTATO HASH:
4. VEGETABLE STIR-FRY WITH TOFU:
5. SPINACH AND FETA STUFFED CHICKEN BREAST:
6. TURKEY AND VEGETABLE CHILI:
7. WHOLE GRAIN PASTA WITH PESTO AND VEGGIES:
8. BAKED COD WITH QUINOA PILAF:
9. BUTTERNUT SQUASH AND LENTIL CURRY
10. GRILLED CHICKEN AND VEGETABLE KEBABS

Chapter 5: Bonus
Smoothies Recipes

1. BANANA PEANUT BUTTER BLISS:
2. CHOCOLATE AVOCADO DELIGHT:
3. MANGO COCONUT DREAM
4. VANILLA ALMOND POWERHOUSE
5. STRAWBERRY BANANA BLISS
6. PINEAPPLE SPINACH SMOOTHIE:
7. BLUEBERRY ALMOND JOY:

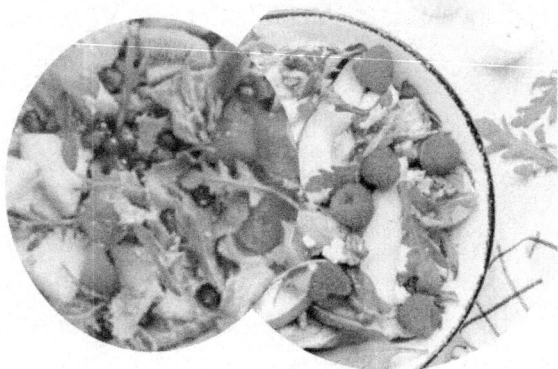

Abstract

Unlock the secrets to healthy and enjoyable weight gain with our specialized cookbook tailored for seniors. This meticulously crafted collection of recipes goes beyond mere calorie counting, prioritizing nutrient-rich ingredients to support overall well-being.

Embracing the unique dietary needs of seniors, each recipe is thoughtfully designed to enhance flavor, texture, and nutritional density. From delectable high-calorie snacks to nourishing main courses, this cookbook offers a diverse range of options that cater to various taste preferences and dietary restrictions.

With a focus on promoting muscle mass, bone health, and energy levels, our cookbook provides seniors with the tools to achieve sustainable weight gain and improved vitality. Embrace a delicious journey towards a healthier and more robust lifestyle, celebrating the joy of food while prioritizing the nutritional needs of our cherished seniors."

Introduction

Jasmine, a vibrant retiree with a passion for cooking, stumbled upon a peculiar book titled "Weight Gain Cookbook for Seniors." Initially skeptical, she embraced the challenge of turning nutritional recipes into delectable delights. As she embarked on this culinary journey, Jasmine not only mastered the art of creating savory, health-conscious meals but also discovered a newfound community of like-minded seniors online.

Her kitchen became a laboratory, experimenting with wholesome ingredients that transformed into mouthwatering dishes. Word spread about Jasmine's culinary prowess, attracting seniors from the neighborhood to join her cooking sessions. The cookbook, initially perceived as an oddity, became a catalyst for a vibrant social circle, fostering friendships and well-being.

Jasmine's journey showcased the transformative power of embracing change, turning a seemingly niche cookbook into a recipe for a fulfilling and connected retirement. Her story became an inspiration for seniors nationwide, proving that age is no barrier to culinary innovation and community building.

CHAPTER 1

How to follow weight gain cookbook

Examine the Cookbook: Begin by reading the weight gain cookbook for seniors. Prepare yourself by familiarizing yourself with the recipes, ingredients, and portion sizes.

Consult an expert: Before making major dietary changes, it's a good idea to consult with a healthcare expert or a nutritionist. They can give you specific advise depending on your health and nutritional requirements.

Understand Caloric Needs: Seniors may have varying caloric requirements. Check if the cookbook meets your specific needs for healthy weight gain. Consider your exercise level, metabolism, and any underlying health issues.

Look for meals that provide a balance of macronutrients (carbohydrates, proteins, and fats) and micronutrients (vitamins and minerals). A well-balanced diet is critical for general health.

Meal Planning: Make a meal plan based on the cookbook's recommendations. Include a variety of foods to receive a wide range of nutrients. To avoid overeating, pay attention to portion proportions.

Regular Eating Schedule: Aim for consistent and regular meal times. This helps to regulate your metabolism and guarantees a consistent calorie intake throughout the day.

Hydration: Don't overlook the significance of being hydrated. Water is essential for general health and might aid digestion.

Adapt to Preferences: Change recipes to suit your tastes, dietary constraints, or allergies. The cookbook should be used as a reference, and it's fine to make changes to fit your specific needs.

Keep Track of Your Progress: Keep track of your weight increase progress. If you are not getting the expected outcomes or are experiencing any side effects, speak with a healthcare expert for assistance.

Other Lifestyle Factors: Take into account other lifestyle factors such as exercise and sleep. Regular physical activity can help with a healthy weight growth process, and proper sleep is essential for overall health.

CHAPTER 2

Flavorful And Calorie- Dense Breakfast Recipes Booster

1. Oatmeal Peanut Porridge

Ingredients:

- pound rolled oats
- cups milk (or a dairy-free substitute)
- 2 tbsp of peanut butter
- 1 tbsp honey or maple syrup (optional, for added sweetness)
- a quarter teaspoon of salt a half teaspoon of vanilla extract
- Optional toppings: sliced bananas, chopped almonds, or berries

Preparation:

1. Combine the rolled oats, milk, peanut butter, salt, and vanilla extract in a saucepan.

2. Cook, stirring constantly, over medium heat until the mixture comes to a boil.

3. Reduce the heat to low and gently simmer for 5-7 minutes, or until the oats are cooked and the porridge has achieved the consistency you prefer. Stir every now and again.

4. If using, sweeten with honey or maple syrup and season with salt to taste.

5. Remove from the fire and set aside for one minute to thicken.

6. If desired, top the oatmeal with sliced bananas, chopped almonds, or berries.

Nutritional Value:

- This meal contains a healthy balance of carbohydrates, protein, and fats.
- High in fiber, oats give you sustained energy.

- Peanut butter provides protein as well as beneficial fats. Milk provides calcium as well as added protein.

Cooking Time:

Approximately 10-15 minutes.

2. Sausage And Cheese Omelet

Ingredients:

- 3huge eggs a quarter cup milk
- 1/2 cup crumbled cooked sausage a half-cup crumbled cheddar cheese
- Season to taste with salt and pepper.
- 1 tablespoon melted butter

Preparation:

1. In a mixing bowl, whisk together the eggs and milk until well combined.

2. Combine the crumbled sausage and shredded cheddar cheese in a mixing bowl. Season with salt and pepper to taste.

3. Melt and heat the butter in a nonstick skillet over medium heat. Pour the egg mixture into the skillet, spreading it evenly.

4. Allow the edges to set before carefully lifting them to allow the uncooked eggs to pour beneath.

5. Fold the omelet in half with a spatula once it is mostly set but still somewhat runny on top.

6. Cook for 1 minute more, or until the cheese melts and the eggs are fully cooked. Place the omelet on a platter and serve immediately.

Nutritional Value

- 450 kcal is the approximate number of calories.
- 25g protein

- Fat: 35g
- 3g carbohydrate 0g fiber

Cooking Time:

Preparation: 5 minutes

Cooking: 8-10 minutes

3. Delicious Mango Shake

Ingredients:

- 2 peeled and chopped ripe mangoes
- cup ice cold milk
- 1/2 cup unsweetened yogurt
- tbsp honey or sugar (modify according to taste) a half teaspoon of vanilla extract Ice cubes are optional. Optional garnish: mint leaves

Preparation:

1. Combine the chopped mangoes, cool milk, plain yogurt, honey or sugar, and vanilla extract in a blender.

2. Blend until the mixture is smooth and creamy.

3. If you want a thicker consistency, add a couple ice cubes and blend again.

4. Adjust the sweetness of the smoothie as needed by adding extra honey or sugar.

5. Fill glasses halfway with mango shake.

6. If desired, garnish with mint leaves. Serve right away and enjoy!

Nutritional Value:

- Mangoes are high in vitamins A and C, which act as antioxidants and immune boosters.

- Milk and yogurt give calcium and protein to the drink.

- Honey provides natural sweetness as well as potential health advantages.

- The smoothie provides energy and might be a refreshing snack.

Cooking Time:

Preparation takes approximately 10 minutes, making this mango shake a quick and delightful treat.

4. Homemade Granola Breakfast

Ingredients:

- 3 cups rolled oats, old-fashioned
- 1 cup chopped nuts (almonds, walnuts, or other)
- 1/2 cup seeds (either sunflower or pumpkin)
- 1/2 cup maple syrup or honey 1/4 cup melted coconut oil a tsp vanilla extract 1/2 teaspoon cinnamon powder
- 1 teaspoon of salt
- Optional: 1 cup dried fruits (raisins, cranberries, or apricots)

Preparation:

1. Preheat the oven to 325 degrees Fahrenheit (163 degrees Celsius).

2. Combine the rolled oats, chopped nuts, and seeds in a large mixing bowl.

3. Whisk together the honey or maple syrup, melted coconut oil, vanilla essence, ground cinnamon, and salt in a separate bowl.

4. Stir the wet mixture into the dry ingredients until completely incorporated.

5. Spread the mixture evenly on a baking sheet lined with parchment paper.

6. Bake for 20-25 minutes, stirring halfway through, or until the granola is golden brown and crisp.

7. Remove from the oven and set aside on the baking sheet to cool completely.

8. If desired, add dried fruits after it has cooled.

Nutritional Value:

- This recipe yields around 6 cups of granola.
- Nutritional values may vary depending on the ingredients utilized.
- Approximately 250 calories, 5g protein, 12g fat, 30g carbs, and 4g fiber per 1/2 cup serving.

Cooking Time:

Approximately 20-25 minutes.

5. Cottage Cheese Pancake With Raspberry Jelly

Ingredients:

- 1 pound of ricotta cheese
- 1 pound cottage cheese
- 1 tablespoon all-purpose flour 1 tablespoon baking powder a quarter teaspoon of salt
- 1 egg a quarter cup milk 1 tbsp. vegetable oil 14 cup raspberry jam

Preparation:

1. In a large mixing bowl, combine the ricotta cheese, cottage cheese, flour, baking powder, and salt.
2. In a separate bowl, whisk together the egg and milk.
3. Combine the wet and dry ingredients until just combined.
4. Warm the vegetable oil in a large skillet over medium heat.
5. Pour 1/4 cup batter into the skillet for each pancake.
6. Cook for 2 to 3 minutes per side, or until golden brown. Serve immediately with raspberry jelly.

Nutritional Value:

- Serving size:
- 240 calories

- 8 gram fat
- 32 gram carbohydrate
- 16 grams of protein
- Fiber: 2 g

Cooking Time:

About 15 minutes

Here are some other tips for making cottage cheese pancakes:

You can use whole-wheat flour instead of all-purpose flour for a more nutritious pancake.

If you don't have raspberry jelly, you can use any other type of jelly or jam that you like. You can also serve these pancakes with fresh fruit, such as berries or bananas.

6. Full English Breakfast

Ingredients:

Bacon:

- Roughly 4-6 rashers per person Grill or fried till golden brown.

Sausages:

- Approximately 2-3 per person Grill or fry until thoroughly done.

Eggs:

- 2 pieces per person
- Cooking methods: fried or poached

Chocolate Pudding:

- 2 slices for each person Fry until well hot and crispy.

Tomatoes:

- 2 portions for each individual
- Grill until slightly softened before serving.

Mushrooms:

- A handful for each person Sautéed in butter till golden brown

Beans Baked:

- cup to 1/2 cup per person Heat in a saucepan or in the microwave.

Breakfast Hash Browns:

- pieces per person
- Fry till golden brown and crunchy.

Toast:

- 2 slices for each person
- Toast the bread till golden brown.
- Quantity of butter: to taste Spread on toast to prepare

Cooking preparation:

Start with the Bacon and Sausages:

- Cook them in a grill or frying pan until they reach your desired level of crispiness.

Prepare Eggs:

- Fry or poach eggs according to your preference.

Cook Black Pudding:

- Fry slices until they are heated through and have a crispy exterior.

Grill Tomatoes:

- Halve tomatoes and grill until slightly softened.

Sauté Mushrooms:

- Cook mushrooms in butter until golden.

Heat Baked Beans:

- Warm beans in a saucepan or microwave.

Fry Hash Browns:

- Cook hash browns until golden and crispy.

Toast Bread:

- Toast slices until golden brown.

Serve Warm:

- Arrange all of the ingredients on a platter and serve immediately.

Nutritional Value:

- Nutritional content varies depending on brand and preparation method. A Full English Breakfast often contains a significant quantity of protein, healthy fats, vitamins, and minerals. However, because it is a filling and calorie-dense dinner, it is best consumed in moderation.

Cooking Time:

Cooking times vary, but on average, a Full English Breakfast takes about 20-30 minutes to prepare, depending on your multitasking abilities and cooking methods.

7. Quick Peanut Butter And Jam Sandwich

Ingredients:

- 2 slices bread (white, whole wheat, sourdough, etc.)
- 2 tbsp. smooth peanut butter
- 2 tbsp fruit jelly or jam (whatever flavor you choose!)

Preparation:

1. One slice of bread, evenly spread with peanut butter.
2. On the other slice of bread, equally spread the jelly or jam.

3. To make the sandwich, press the two slices of bread together.

Nutritional Value:

per sandwich):

- Calories: About 300-350, depending on the bread and spreads used.
- 10-15 grams of fat
- 35-40 grams of carbohydrates
- 8 to 10 g protein

Cooking time:

- This sandwich cooks in no time! It's ready to use as soon as you put it together.

Tips:

Use softened peanut butter for a creamier sandwich. If you're feeling daring, top your sandwich with sliced bananas or strawberries. To prepare a grilled

PB&J, smear a small layer of butter on the outside of each bread slice before grilling till golden brown and crispy in a skillet or griddle over medium heat.

8. Vegan Protein Shake

Ingredients:

- 1 quart almond milk
- 1 scoop protein powder made from plants
- 1 tbsp. almond butter a half banana a half teaspoon cinnamon Ice cubes are optional.

Preparation:

1. 1 cup almond milk is combined in a blender.
2. 1 scoop of your favorite plant-based protein powder.
3. 1 tablespoon almond butter is added for creaminess.
4. 1/2 banana, sliced, should be added to the blender.

5. To add taste, add 1/2 teaspoon cinnamon.

6. Add ice cubes if you want your shake to be cooler.

7. Blend until a creamy, smooth consistency is achieved.

8. Pour into a glass and serve.

Nutritional Value:

- Protein: This varies depending on the protein powder (usually 20-25g).

- Calories: Around 300-350 calories

- Almond butter contains healthy lipids.

- Bananas provide potassium and fiber.

Cooking Time:

5 minutes

Adjust ingredient quantities based on personal preferences and dietary needs.

9. Tofu Scramble

Ingredients:

- 1 firm tofu block (14-16 ounces)
- 1 tablespoon oil (olive oil, vegetable oil, or any oil of choice)
- 1/2 diced onion
- diced bell pepper
- minced garlic cloves
- 1 tsp turmeric powder (to add color) a half teaspoon cumin powder paprika, 1/2 teaspoon
- Season with salt and pepper to taste.
- Spinach, tomatoes, nutritional yeast, or additional veggies and seasonings of your choice are optional.

Preparation:

1. Press the tofu to extract any excess water. Cut it into little, palatable bits.

2. In a big skillet, warm the oil over medium heat.
3. Mix in the diced onions, bell peppers, and garlic. Cook until softened.
4. Stir in the crumbled tofu with the vegetables in the skillet.
5. Sprinkle the tofu mixture with turmeric, cumin, paprika, salt, and pepper. Stir well to coat the tofu evenly.
6. If you're using extra vegetables, add them to the skillet and sauté until they're soft.
7. Cook for 8-10 minutes, stirring periodically, until the tofu scramble is heated through and slightly crunchy.
8. Season with salt and pepper to taste.

Nutritional Value:

- Tofu is high in plant-based protein, with roughly 10-15 grams per 3-ounce serving.

- Bell peppers include vitamin C as well as other antioxidants.

- Onions and garlic add flavor as well as potential health advantages.

Cooking Time:

Approximately 20 minutes.

10. Avocado And Egg Sandwich

Ingredients:

- 2 slices whole-wheat bread 1 avocado, ripe two huge eggs

- Season with salt and pepper to taste.

- Optional garnishes include sliced tomatoes, arugula, and spicy sauce.

Preparation:

1. Toast the whole-grain bread pieces to taste.
2. While the bread toasts, cut the ripe avocado in half, remove the pit, and scoop out the meat.
3. With a fork, mash the avocado until smooth.
4. Fry the eggs to your liking (fried, scrambled, or poached) in a nonstick pan over medium heat.
5. Season with salt and pepper to taste.
6. On one side of each toasted bread piece, evenly spread the mashed avocado.
7. On one slice of bread, place the cooked eggs on top of the mashed avocado.
8. Optional garnishes include sliced tomatoes, arugula, and a splash of spicy sauce.
9. Place the second slice of toasted bread, avocado side down, on top. Serve the sandwich immediately cut in half.

Nutritional Value (Estimated):

- 450-500 kilocalories

- Protein content: 20-25g

- Fat: 25-30g

- 40-45g carbohydrate Fiber content: 10-12g

Time to Cook:

Approximately 10-15 minutes

CHAPTER 3

Delectable Lunch Recipes To Put On Weight

1. Chicken and Quinoa Salad

Ingredients:

- quinoa cup
- c. water
- pound skinless boneless chicken breasts Season with salt and pepper to taste.
- tbsp of olive oil
- 1 diced red bell pepper 1 diced cucumber
- cup halved cherry tomatoes
- 1/4 cup finely chopped red onion
- 1/4 cup crumbled feta cheese 1/4 cup chopped fresh parsley

To make the dressing:

- three tbsp olive oil

- tbsp of lemon juice
- 1 teaspoon Dijon mustard 1 minced garlic clove Season with salt and pepper to taste.

Preparation:

1. Rinse the quinoa with cool water. Combine quinoa and water in a saucepan. Bring to a boil, then lower to a low heat, cover, and leave to simmer for 15-20 minutes, or until the water has been absorbed. Allow to cool after fluffing with a fork.

2. Season the chicken breasts with salt and pepper. In a medium-high heat pan, warm the olive oil. Cook for 6-8 minutes per side, or until the chicken is done. Allow to cool before slicing.

3. Combine cooked quinoa, diced chicken, bell pepper, cucumber, cherry tomatoes, red onion, feta cheese, and parsley in a large mixing bowl.

4. Whisk together the dressing ingredients in a small bowl: olive oil, lemon juice, Dijon mustard, minced garlic, salt, and pepper.

5. Toss the salad with the dressing to mix. If necessary, adjust the seasoning.

Per Serving Nutritional Value:

- 400 calories
- 25g protein
- 30g carbohydrates
- Fat: 20g
- 4g fiber
- 3g sugar

Cooking Time: Approximately 30 minutes

2. Sweet Potato and Black Bean Bowl:

Ingredients:

- 2 medium-sized peeled and sliced sweet potatoes
- 1 can (15 oz) washed and drained black beans
- 1 quinoa cup
- chopped red bell pepper
- 1/2 coarsely chopped red onion
- minced garlic cloves
- 1 tablespoon extra virgin olive oil
- 1 tablespoon cumin 1 tablespoon chili powder Season with salt and pepper to taste. Garnish with fresh cilantro

Preparation:

1. Rinse 1 cup of quinoa under cold water to prepare.
2. Combine the quinoa and 2 cups of water in a saucepan.

3. Bring to a boil, then reduce to a low heat, cover, and cook for 15-20 minutes, or until the quinoa is tender and the water has been absorbed.

4. Preheat the oven to 400°F (200°C) for roasting sweet potatoes.

5. Toss the sweet potatoes in a bowl with the olive oil, cumin, chili powder, salt, and pepper. Roast for 25-30 minutes, or until tender and slightly crispy, on a baking sheet.

6. Sauté the red bell pepper, red onion, and garlic in a skillet until softened.

7. In a large mixing bowl, combine the cooked quinoa, roasted sweet potatoes, sautéed veggies, and black beans.

8. Seasoning: To taste, adjust the salt, pepper, and extra spices.

9. Before serving, garnish with fresh cilantro.

Nutritional Value (Estimated):

- 400 calories per serving
- 12g protein
- 75g carbohydrate
- 12g dietary fiber
- Fat: 8g
- Vitamin A: 400% DV
- Vitamin C: 90% of the DV Iron: 15% of the daily

Cooking Time:

Quinoa: 15-20 minutes

Roasting Sweet Potatoes: 25-30 minutes

Enjoy your nutritious Sweet Potato and Black Bean Bowl!

3. Salmon and Vegetable Stir-Fry

Ingredients:

- pound (450g) cut into cubes salmon fillets
- tbsp of soy sauce
- 1 teaspoon oyster sauce
- tbsp sesame seed oil
- tbsp of vegetable oil
- minced garlic cloves
- 1 tablespoon grated ginger
- 1 finely sliced red bell pepper
- 1 finely sliced yellow bell pepper
- 1 cup broccoli florets (150g)
- 1 julienned carrot
- sliced zucchini 1 cup (150g) snap peas
- sliced green onions
- Serve with cooked rice or noodles.

Preparation:

1. In a mixing bowl, combine the soy sauce, oyster sauce, and sesame oil. Marinate the salmon cubes for about 15 minutes in this mixture.

2. In a large wok or skillet, heat the vegetable oil over medium-high heat..

3. Stir in the minced garlic and grated ginger for about 30 seconds, or until fragrant.

4. Cook for 2-3 minutes, or until the marinated salmon cubes are browned on all sides. Set aside the fish from the wok.

5. Stir-fry the sliced bell peppers, broccoli, carrot, zucchini, and snap peas in the same wok for 3-4 minutes, or until the veggies are crisp-tender.

6. Return the cooked salmon to the wok, add the sliced green onions, and stir for another 2 minutes.

7. Serve the stir-fry with rice or noodles.

Nutritional Value:

- Approximately 400 calories per serving
- 30g protein, 20g fat
- 25g carbohydrate 5g fiber

Cooking Time:

Preparation: 20 minutes

Cooking: 10 minutes

Total: 30 minutes

4. Mushroom and Spinach Omelette:

Ingredients:

- two huge eggs
- 1/2 cup sliced mushrooms 1 cup chopped fresh spinach 1/4 cup finely diced onion
- Optional: 1/4 cup shredded cheese Season with salt and pepper to taste. 1 tablespoon extra virgin olive oil

Nutritional Value:

- Eggs are high in protein, vitamins, and minerals.
- Mushrooms are low in calories, high in antioxidants, and high in vitamins.
- Spinach is high in vitamins A and C, as well as iron and fiber.
- Cheese: Calcium and protein are added by cheese.

Preparation:

1. In a nonstick skillet over medium heat, heat the olive oil.
2. Sauté the onions until they are transparent.
3. Cook until the mushrooms release moisture and turn golden brown.
4. Cook for 5 minutes, or until the spinach is wilted.

5. Whisk the eggs in a mixing bowl and season with salt and pepper.

6. Over the mushroom and spinach mixture, pour the beaten eggs.

7. Allow the eggs to set around the edges before lifting and tilting the pan gently to allow the uncooked eggs to flow to the edges.

8. Optional: Sprinkle the omelette with shredded cheese.

9. Fold the omelette in half using a spatula once the eggs are mostly set.

10. Cook for another minute, or until the cheese (if used) is melted and the eggs are fully cooked.

Cooking Time:

Approximately 8-10 minutes.

5. Pasta Primavera with Grilled Chicken:

Ingredients:

- 8 ounces (225g) of your preferred pasta
- 2 skinless, boneless chicken breasts
- 2 tbsp of olive oil
- 1 cup halved cherry tomatoes
- 1 cup florets broccoli
- 1 medium-sized sliced zucchini
- 1 medium-sized julienned carrot
- 1/2 cup finely sliced bell peppers
- 3 minced garlic cloves

Season with salt and pepper to taste.

- 1/2 cup Parmesan cheese, grated
- Garnish with fresh basil or parsley

For the marinade for the chicken:

- 2 tbsp of olive oil
- 1 teaspoon Italian dried herbs

- 1 tsp. garlic powder
- Season with salt and pepper to taste.

Preparation:

1. Marinate the chicken by combining olive oil, dried Italian herbs, garlic powder, salt, and pepper in a mixing bowl.
2. Allow the chicken breasts to marinate in the marinade for at least 30 minutes.
3. Prepare the Pasta: Cook the pasta according to package directions until al dente. Set aside after draining.
4. Preheat the grill or grill pan over medium-high heat before grilling the chicken.
5. Grill the marinated chicken breasts for 6-8 minutes per side, or until cooked through. Allow for a few minutes of rest before slicing the chicken into strips.

Make the Vegetables:

1. Warm the olive oil in a large saucepan over medium heat.
2. Sauté the minced garlic until fragrant.
3. Broccoli, zucchini, carrots, and bell peppers are optional. Cook for 5-7 minutes, or until the vegetables are soft but crunchy.
4. Cook for a further 2-3 minutes after adding the cherry tomatoes.
5. Combine and serve: Add the cooked pasta and vegetables to the pan.
6. Toss everything together in a large mixing bowl, sprinkle with olive oil, and season with salt & pepper to taste.
7. Place the grilled chicken slices on top.
8. Sprinkle with Parmesan cheese and garnish with fresh basil or parsley.

Nutritional Value:

- The nutritional content will vary depending on the brands and quantity of the ingredients used. In general, this dish has a lot of protein from the chicken, fiber from the vegetables, and carbohydrates from the pasta.

Cooking Time:

- Approximately 30-40 minutes, including marinating time.Quinoa and Chickpea Stuffed Peppers:

Bell peppers stuffed with a mixture of quinoa, chickpeas, diced tomatoes, and spices, baked to perfection.

6. Turkey and Veggie Wrap:

Ingredients:

- 1 large whole-wheat wrap
- 4 oz. sliced turkey breast 1/2 cup lettuce, shredded a quarter cup chopped tomatoes
- 1/4 cup cucumber slices 1/4 cup carrots, shredded hummus (two tablespoons)
- 1 tbsp (optional) Greek yogurt

Preparation:

1. Season with salt and pepper to taste.
2. Lay the whole-grain wrap flat on a clean surface to prepare.
3. Spread hummus evenly throughout the wrap.
4. Arrange the turkey breast slices in the center of the wrap.
5. Sprinkle the turkey with shredded lettuce, chopped tomatoes, sliced cucumbers, and shredded carrots.

6. Add a spoonful of Greek yogurt for added richness if desired.

7. Season to taste with salt and pepper.

8. Fold in the sides of the wrap carefully, then roll it tightly from the bottom to create a secure wrap.

Nutritional Value:

- Calories: Around 350-400 kcal

- Protein content: 20-25g

- 40-45g carbohydrate

- Fat: 12-15g Fiber content: 6-8g

Cooking Time:

No cooking required; preparation time is around 10 minutes.

7. Bean and Lentil Soup:

Bean Soup:

Ingredients:

- 1 cup dry beans (any kind, such as navy beans or black beans)
- chopped onion 2 diced carrots
- celery stalks, chopped 3 garlic cloves, minced
- 6 cups broth (vegetable or chicken) 1 teaspoon thyme dried one bay leaf
- Season with salt and pepper to taste. Cooking with olive oil

Preparation:

1. Rinse the beans and soak them overnight. Before using, drain.
2. Sauté onions, carrots, and celery in olive oil in a large pot until softened.
3. Cook for another minute after adding the garlic.

56

4. To the pot, add the soaked beans, broth, thyme, bay leaf, salt, and pepper.
5. Bring to a boil, then reduce to a low heat and continue to cook for 1.5 to 2 hours, or until the beans are soft.
6. Before serving, remove the bay leaf.

Nutritional Value:

- Protein and fiber content is high.
- Vitamin and mineral content is high.
- It is low in fat.

Cooking Time: 1.5 to 2 hours.

Lentil Soup:

Ingredients:

- 1 cup dried lentils (any variety)
- finely chopped onion
- sliced carrots

- 2 celery stalks, chopped 3 garlic cloves, minced
- 6 cups broth (vegetable or chicken)
- 1 teaspoon cumin powder 1 teaspoon cilantro one bay leaf
- Season with salt and pepper to taste Olive oil for sautéing

Preparation:

1. Lentils should be rinsed under cold water.
2. Sauté onions, carrots, and celery in olive oil in a saucepan until softened.
3. Cook for another minute after adding the garlic.
4. Combine the lentils, broth, cumin, coriander, bay leaf, salt, and pepper in a mixing bowl. Bring to a boil, then reduce to a low heat and continue to cook for 25-30 minutes, or until the lentils are cooked.
5. Before serving, remove the bay leaf.

Nutritional Value:

- Excellent source of protein and fiber.
- Rich in iron and folate.
- Low in fat.

Cooking Time: 25-30 minutes.

8. Baked Cod with Roasted Vegetables

Ingredients:

- 4 fish fillets (about 6 ounces each)
- 2 tbsp of olive oil
- 2 tablespoons lemon juice 1 teaspoon lemon zest
- 2 minced garlic cloves
- 1 tsp. dried oregano
- Season with salt and pepper to taste.

Vegetables Roasted:

- 1 sliced large zucchini 1 sliced bell pepper 1 sliced red onion

- cup sliced cherry tomatoes
- tbsp of olive oil
- 1 teaspoon thyme dried
- Season with salt and pepper to taste.

preparation

1. Preheat the oven to 400 degrees Fahrenheit (200 degrees Celsius).
2. To make the cod marinade, combine olive oil, lemon zest, lemon juice, chopped garlic, dried oregano, salt, and pepper in a small bowl. Coat the cod fillets with the marinade, making sure they are evenly coated.
3. To make the roasted vegetables, add sliced zucchini, bell pepper, red onion, and cherry tomatoes in a large mixing basin. Drizzle olive oil over the vegetables and season with salt and pepper. To coat, toss with a fork.

4. Assemble and bake: Line a baking sheet with parchment paper and place the marinated fish fillets on it. Arrange the prepared vegetables around the cod. Bake for 20-25 minutes, or until the fish is cooked through and flakes readily with a fork.
5. Serve: Plate the baked cod on a bed of roasted vegetables. Garnish with fresh herbs if desired.

Nutritional Value (per serving):

- Calories: Approximately 350 kcal
- Protein: 30g
- Fat: 18g
- Carbohydrates: 20g
- Fiber: 5g
- Sugars: 8g

Cooking Time: 20-25 minutes

Enjoy your delicious and nutritious Baked Cod with Roasted Vegetables!

9. Greek Yogurt Parfait

Ingredients:

- 1 cup plain Greek yogurt
- 1 granola cup
- 1/2 cup berries (strawberries, blueberries, and raspberries)
- 1 teaspoon honey a quarter teaspoon vanilla extract

Preparation:

1. In a mixing dish, add the Greek yogurt and vanilla essence.
2. Layer the Greek yogurt, granola, and mixed berries in serving glasses or bowls.
3. Repeat the layers until the glass or bowl is full, then top with a layer of berries.

4. Drizzle honey over top for extra sweetness.

Enjoy your tasty Greek Yogurt Parfait right away!

Nutritional Value:

- Calories: About 300 kcal per serving
- 15g protein
- Fat: 8g
- 45g carbohydrate
- 6g fiber 20g of sugar

Cooking Time:

Prep time: 10 minutes

No cooking required

10. Fish and Rice bowl

Ingredients:

- cup steamed jasmine rice
- 1.5 pound fillets of white fish (such as cod or tilapia)
- tbsp of olive oil
- 1 tsp. garlic powder 1 tsp. onion powder
- 1 paprika teaspoon
- Season with salt and pepper to taste.
- 1 cup halved cherry tomatoes
- 1 diced cucumber
- sliced avocado
- tbsp of soy sauce
- 1 tablespoon vinegar (rice)
- 1 teaspoon honey
- Sesame seeds for decoration Garnish with fresh cilantro

Nutritional Value:

- 30g protein per serving
- 5g fiber per serving
- 15g of healthy fat per serving
- Calories: Each serving contains approximately 400 calories.

Preparation:

1. Cook the jasmine rice according per the package directions.
2. Garlic powder, onion powder, paprika, salt, and pepper season the fish fillets.
3. In a large skillet over medium heat, warm the olive oil. Cook the salmon for 3-4 minutes per side, or until done.
4. To make the sauce, combine soy sauce, rice vinegar, and honey in a mixing bowl. Assemble the bowl as follows: Fill each bowl with rice and

top with cooked fish, cherry tomatoes, cucumber, and avocado.

5. Drizzle the sauce over the top of the bowl and top with sesame seeds and fresh cilantro.

Cooking Time:

Rice: 15-20 minutes

Fish: 8-10 minutes

Enjoy your nutritious Fish and Rice Bowl!

CHAPTER 4

Satisfying Dinners Recipes

1. Creamy Chicken Alfredo Pasta:

Ingredients:

- 8 oz (225g) fettuccine pasta
- lb (450g) boneless, skinless chicken breast, cut into strips
- tablespoons olive oil
- 4 cloves garlic, minced
- 1 cup (240ml) heavy cream
- 1 cup (240ml) grated Parmesan cheese
- Salt and pepper to taste
- Fresh parsley, chopped (for garnish)

Preparation:

Cook Pasta:

1. Boil a large pot of salted water.

2. Cook fettuccine pasta according to package instructions until al dente.
3. Drain and set aside.

Cook Chicken:
1. Season the chicken strips with salt and pepper to taste.
2. Warm the olive oil in a large skillet over medium-high heat.
3. Cook until the chicken strips are browned and cooked through.
4. Set aside the chicken from the skillet.

Make the sauce:
1. Sauté the minced garlic in the same skillet until fragrant.
2. Pour in the heavy cream, bring to a simmer, and turn off the heat.

3. Whisk in the Parmesan cheese gradually until the sauce is creamy and thickened. Season to taste with salt and pepper.

Combine and Serve:

1. To the skillet with the Alfredo sauce, add the cooked chicken and drained pasta.
2. Toss everything together until thoroughly coated and hot. Garnish with fresh parsley, if desired.

Nutritional Value:

(These values are approximate and can vary based on specific ingredients and portion sizes)

- Calories: 600 per serving
- Protein: 35g
- Fat: 38g
- Carbohydrates: 35g
- Fiber: 2g

Cooking Time:

Approximately 30 minutes

Enjoy your Creamy Chicken Alfredo Pasta!

2. Quinoa and Black Bean Bowl:

Ingredients:

- cup quinoa
- cups water
- 1 can (15 oz) black beans, drained and rinsed
- 1 cup corn kernels (fresh or frozen)
- 1 cup cherry tomatoes, halved
- avocado, diced
- 1/4 cup red onion, finely chopped
- 1/4 cup cilantro, chopped
- tablespoons olive oil
- 1 lime, juiced
- Salt and pepper to taste

Preparation:

1. Rinse the quinoa under cold water. In a saucepan, combine quinoa and water. Bring to a boil, then reduce heat, cover, and simmer for 15-

20 minutes, or until water is absorbed and quinoa is cooked.

2. Combine cooked quinoa, black beans, corn, cherry tomatoes, avocado, red onion, and cilantro in a large mixing basin.

3. In a small bowl, whisk together olive oil, lime juice, salt, and pepper. Pour the dressing over the quinoa mixture and toss gently to combine.

4. Adjust seasoning to taste and serve immediately.

Nutritional Value (per serving):

- Calories: 400
- Protein: 14g
- Carbohydrates: 60g
- Fiber: 12g
- Fat: 15g
- Saturated Fat: 2g
- Cholesterol: 0mg

- Sodium: 300mg
- Vitamin C: 25%
- Iron: 20%

Cooking Time:

Quinoa: 15-20 minutes

3. Salmon and Sweet Potato Hash:

Ingredients:

- lb fresh salmon fillets, diced
- large sweet potatoes, peeled and diced
- 1 red bell pepper, diced
- yellow onion, finely chopped
- cloves garlic, minced
- 2 tablespoons olive oil
- 1 teaspoon paprika
- 1/2 teaspoon cayenne pepper
- Salt and pepper to taste Fresh parsley for garnish

Preparation:

1. Warm the olive oil in a large skillet over medium heat.

2. Add diced sweet potatoes and cook until slightly tender, stirring occasionally (about 8-10 minutes).

3. Add chopped onion, garlic, and diced bell pepper to the skillet. Cook until the vegetables are softened.

4. Push the vegetables to one side of the skillet and add diced salmon to the empty side. Cook until salmon is cooked through and flakes easily.

5. Combine salmon with the vegetables in the skillet. Add paprika, cayenne pepper, salt, and pepper. Stir well to mix all ingredients.

6. Cook for an additional 3-5 minutes until flavors meld.

7. Garnish with fresh parsley before serving.

Nutritional Value:

Note: Nutritional values can vary depending on the ingredients and portion size.

Salmon is a rich source of omega-3 fatty acids, protein, and vitamin D.

Sweet potatoes provide complex carbohydrates, fiber, and vitamins A and C.

Bell peppers contribute vitamin C and antioxidants.

Olive oil adds healthy fats.

Cooking Time:

Approximately 20-25 minutes from start to finish.

4. Vegetable Stir-Fry with Tofu:

Ingredients:

- block of firm tofu, cubed
- tablespoons soy sauce
- 1 tablespoon sesame oil
- tablespoon vegetable oil
- cloves garlic, minced
- 1 tablespoon ginger, grated
- 1 cup broccoli florets
- 1 bell pepper, thinly sliced
- 1 carrot, julienned
- 1 zucchini, sliced
- cup snap peas, ends trimmed
- green onions, sliced
- 2 tablespoons hoisin sauce
- 1 tablespoon rice vinegar
- 1 teaspoon cornstarch (optional, for thickening)

- Sesame seeds for garnish (optional) Cooked rice or noodles for serving

Preparation:
1. Tofu should be pressed to remove extra water before cutting into cubes.
2. Tofu should be marinated in soy sauce for at least 15 minutes.
3. In a wok or big skillet, heat the vegetable oil over medium-high heat.
4. Stir in the tofu cubes till golden brown. Take out and set aside.
5. Add sesame oil, garlic, and ginger to the same wok. Sauté for a few minutes.
6. Broccoli, bell pepper, carrot, zucchini, and snap peas should all be included. Cook for 5-7 minutes, or until the vegetables are tender-crisp.

7. Return tofu to the wok, add hoisin sauce and rice vinegar. Toss to coat evenly.

8. If desired, mix cornstarch with a bit of water and add to thicken the sauce.

9. Stir in green onions and cook for an additional minute.

10. Garnish with sesame seeds and serve over rice or noodles.

Nutritional Value:

- This dish is rich in protein from tofu and packed with vitamins and fiber from various vegetables. Adjustments to the nutritional content can be made based on specific brands and quantities of ingredients used.

Cooking Time:

Approximately 25-30 minutes, including preparation and cooking. Enjoy your delicious and nutritious Vegetable Stir-Fry with Tofu!

5. Spinach and Feta Stuffed Chicken Breast:

Ingredients:

- 4 boneless, skinless chicken breasts
- 2 cups fresh spinach, chopped
- cup feta cheese, crumbled
- cloves garlic, minced
- 1 tablespoon olive oil
- Salt and pepper to taste
- 1 teaspoon dried oregano
- 1 teaspoon dried thyme Cooking twine (optional)

Preparation:

1. Preheat your oven to 375°F (190°C).

2. In a skillet over medium heat, sauté the chopped spinach and minced garlic in olive oil until the spinach is wilted. Set aside to cool.

3. In a bowl, combine the crumbled feta, dried oregano, and dried thyme.

4. Butterfly each chicken breast by cutting a pocket through the thickest area without cutting all the way through.

5. Sprinkle salt and pepper into each pocket.

6. Stuff each chicken breast with a mixture of sautéed spinach and feta cheese.

7. To keep the stuffing in place, tie the chicken breasts together with cooking twine if preferred.

8. In a baking dish, place the filled chicken breasts.

9. Bake for 25-30 minutes, or until the chicken is cooked through, in a preheated oven.

10.Optional: Broil for an additional 2-3 minutes to brown the top.

Nutritional Value (per serving):
- Calories: Approximately 350 kcal
- Protein: Approximately 40g
- Fat: Approximately 18g
- Carbohydrates: Approximately 5g Fiber: Approximately 2g

Cooking Time:

Prep Time: 15 minutes

Cooking Time: 25-30 minutes

Enjoy your Spinach and Feta Stuffed Chicken Breast!

6. Turkey and Vegetable Chili:

Ingredients:

- 1 lb ground turkey
- 1 tablespoon olive oil
- onion, diced
- bell peppers, diced
- carrots, diced
- cloves garlic, minced
- 1 can (15 oz) diced tomatoes
- 1 can (15 oz) black beans, drained and rinsed
- 1 can (15 oz) kidney beans, drained and rinsed
- 1 cup corn kernels (fresh or frozen)
- cup chicken broth
- tablespoons chili powder
- 1 teaspoon cumin
- 1 teaspoon paprika Salt and pepper to taste

Preparation:

1. Warm the olive oil in a big pot over medium heat. Cook until the ground turkey is browned.
2. Mix in the diced onion, bell peppers, carrots, and garlic. Cook until the vegetables are tender. Combine chopped tomatoes, black beans, kidney beans, corn, and chicken broth in a mixing bowl.
3. Chili powder, cumin, paprika, salt, and pepper to taste. Combine thoroughly.
4. Bring the chili to a boil, then reduce to a low heat and continue to cook for 20-25 minutes, stirring regularly.

Nutritional Value:

- Serving Size: 1 cup
- Calories: 250
- Protein: 20g

- Carbohydrates: 30g
- Fiber: 8g
- Fat: 7g

Cooking Time: 20-25 minutes

7. Whole Grain Pasta with Pesto and Veggies:

Ingredients:

- 8 ounces whole grain pasta
- 2 cups mixed vegetables (e.g., cherry tomatoes, broccoli, bell peppers)
- 1/2 cup basil pesto
- 2 tablespoons olive oil
- 2 cloves garlic, minced
- Salt and pepper to taste
- Grated Parmesan cheese for serving (optional

Preparation:

Cook Pasta:

- Bring a big saucepan of water to a boil and season with salt.
- Cook the whole grain pasta until al dente according to package directions. Set aside after draining.

Prepare Vegetables:

- While the pasta cooks, heat the olive oil in a skillet over medium heat.
- Sauté the minced garlic until fragrant.
- Cook the mixed veggies until they are tender-crisp.

Combine Pasta and Veggies:

- Mix the cooked pasta with the sautéed vegetables in the pan.

Add Pesto:

- Stir in the basil pesto until the pasta and vegetables are evenly coated. Season to taste with salt and pepper.

Serve:

- Serve the whole grain spaghetti with pesto and vegetables on individual plates. Optionally, top with grated Parmesan cheese for extra flavor.

Nutritional Value:

- This meal is high in whole grains, which provide complex carbohydrates and fiber.
- The mixed vegetables provide important vitamins and minerals.
- Basil pesto contains healthful fats, namely olive oil and pine nuts.

Cooking Time:

Approximately 20-25 minutes, depending on the pasta cooking time and vegetable tenderness. Enjoy your wholesome and nutritious Whole Grain Pasta with Pesto and Veggies!

8. Baked Cod with Quinoa Pilaf:

Baked Cod:

Ingredients:

- 4 cod fillets (about 6 ounces each)
- 2 tablespoons olive oil
- lemon (juiced)
- cloves garlic (minced)
- 1 teaspoon dried oregano Salt and pepper to taste

Preparation:

1. Preheat the oven to 375°F (190°C).
2. In a baking dish, place the fish fillets.

3. Combine the olive oil, lemon juice, minced garlic, dried oregano, salt, and pepper in a small mixing bowl.

4. Pour the mixture over the cod fillets and coat thoroughly.

5. Bake the fish for 15-20 minutes, or until it flakes easily with a fork.

Nutritional Value (per serving):

- Calories: 250
- Protein: 30g
- Fat: 12g Carbohydrates: 3g

Quinoa Pilaf:

Ingredients:

- cup quinoa
- cups chicken or vegetable broth
- 1 tablespoon olive oil
- onion (finely chopped)

- carrots (diced)
- 1 bell pepper (diced)
- 1/2 cup peas
- Salt and pepper to taste Fresh parsley for garnish

Preparation:

1. Rinse the quinoa with cool water.
2. Warm the olive oil in a saucepan and sauté the onion until transparent.
3. Toast the quinoa in the pot for 2 minutes.
4. Bring to a boil with the broth. Reduce the heat to low, cover, and leave to simmer for 15 minutes.
5. Cook carrots, bell pepper, and peas separately until soft.
6. Combine the cooked quinoa and the sautéed vegetables in a mixing bowl. Season with salt and pepper to taste.
7. Before serving, garnish with fresh parsley.

Nutritional Value (per serving):

- Calories: 180
- Protein: 5g
- Fat: 5g
- Carbohydrates: 30g

Cooking Time:

- Baked Cod: 15-20 minutes
- Quinoa Pilaf: 25 minutes

Enjoy your delicious and nutritious meal!

9. Butternut Squash and Lentil Curry

Ingredients:

- 1 medium-sized butternut squash, peeled, seeded, and diced
- 1 cup dry lentils (red or green), rinsed
- 1 onion, finely chopped
- 3 cloves garlic, minced

- 1 can (14 oz) diced tomatoes
- can (14 oz) coconut milk
- tablespoons curry powder
- 1 teaspoon ground cumin
- 1 teaspoon ground coriander
- 1 teaspoon turmeric
- teaspoon paprika
- Salt and pepper to taste
- tablespoons vegetable oil
- Fresh cilantro for garnish (optional) Cooked rice for serving

Preparation:

1. Warm the vegetable oil in a big pot over medium heat. Sauté the chopped onions and minced garlic until softened.

2. Mix in the curry powder, cumin, coriander, turmeric, and paprika. To coat the onions and garlic with the spices, stir well.

3. Pour in the cubed butternut squash and washed lentils. To combine with the spice mixture, stir well.

4. Combine the diced tomatoes and coconut milk in a mixing bowl. Season to taste with salt and pepper. To incorporate all of the ingredients, stir them together.

5. Bring the curry to a boil, then lower to a low heat, cover, and continue to cook for 25-30 minutes, or until the butternut squash and lentils are cooked.

6. While the curry is cooking, make the rice according to package directions.

7. When the curry is done, taste it and adjust the seasoning as needed. Serve the stew over cooked rice, if desired garnished with fresh cilantro.

Nutritional Value:

- This curry is a good source of fiber, protein, vitamins (especially vitamin A from butternut squash), and healthy fats from coconut milk.

Cooking Time:

Approximately 45-50 minutes (including preparation and simmering time).

10. Grilled Chicken and Vegetable Kebabs

Ingredients:

- 1 pound (about 450g) boneless, skinless chicken breasts, cut into 1-inch cubes
- 1 large bell pepper, cut into chunks
- 1 zucchini, sliced into rounds
- red onion, cut into wedges
- Cherry tomatoes (optional) Wooden or metal skewers

Marinade:

- 1/4 cup (60ml) olive oil
- tablespoons soy sauce
- 2 cloves garlic, minced
- 1 teaspoon dried oregano
- 1 teaspoon paprika Salt and pepper to taste

Preparation:

Prepare Marinade:

1. Whisk together olive oil, soy sauce, minced garlic, oregano, paprika, salt, and pepper in a mixing bowl.
2. Marinate the chicken by placing it in a resealable plastic bag or shallow dish.
3. Pour half of the marinade over the chicken, coating each piece thoroughly.

4. Refrigerate for at least 30 minutes (or overnight for added taste) after sealing the bag or covering the dish.

Prepare Vegetables:
- In a separate bowl, toss bell pepper, zucchini, and red onion with the remaining marinade.

Preheat Grill:
Preheat your grill to medium-high heat.

Assemble Kebabs:
Thread marinated chicken, bell pepper, zucchini, red onion, and cherry tomatoes onto skewers, alternating ingredients.

Grill Kebabs:

- Place the kebabs on the hot grill.
- Grill, rotating periodically, for 10-15 minutes, or until chicken is cooked through and veggies are soft.

Serve:

- Remove the kebabs from the grill and set them aside for a few minutes to rest.
- Garnish with fresh herbs if desired and serve hot.

Nutritional Value (Approximate):

- Calories: Varies based on specific ingredients and serving size.
- Protein: High due to chicken.
- Healthy fats: Olive oil provides healthy fats.
- Vitamins and Minerals: Abundant in vegetables.

Cooking Time:

Marinating: 30 minutes to overnight

Grilling: 10-15 minutes

Enjoy your delicious Grilled Chicken and Vegetable Kebabs!

CHAPTER 5: BONUS

Smoothies Recipes

1. Banana Peanut Butter Bliss:

Ingredients: 2 ripe bananas, 2 tablespoons peanut butter, 1 cup milk (dairy or plant-based), ice cubes.

Preparation: Blend all ingredients until smooth.

Nutritional Value: Rich in potassium and protein.

Cooking Time: 5 minutes.

2. Chocolate Avocado Delight:

Ingredients: 1 ripe avocado, 2 tablespoons cocoa powder, 1 tablespoon honey, 1 cup almond milk, ice cubes.

Preparation: Blend until creamy.

Nutritional Value: High in healthy fats and antioxidants.

Cooking Time: 5 minutes.

3. Mango Coconut Dream

Ingredients: 1 cup mango chunks, 1/2 cup coconut milk, 1/2 cup Greek yogurt, 1 tablespoon chia seeds, ice cubes.

Preparation: Blend until smooth.

Nutritional Value: Packed with vitamins and probiotics. Cooking Time: 5 minutes.

4. Vanilla Almond Powerhouse

Ingredients: 1 teaspoon vanilla extract, 1/4 cup almonds, 1 banana, 1 cup milk (dairy or plant-based), ice cubes.

Preparation: Blend all ingredients until creamy.

Nutritional Value: Good source of protein and vitamin E.

Cooking Time: 5 minutes.

5. Strawberry Banana Bliss

Ingredients: 1 cup strawberries, 1 banana, 1/2 cup yogurt, 1 cup orange juice, ice cubes.

Preparation: Blend until well combined.

Nutritional Value: High in vitamin C and potassium. Cooking Time: 5 minutes.

6. Pineapple Spinach Smoothie:

Ingredients: 1 cup pineapple chunks, 1 cup spinach leaves, 1/2 cucumber, 1/2 cup coconut water, ice cubes.

Preparation: Blend until smooth.

Nutritional Value: Packed with vitamins and minerals.

Cooking Time: 5 minutes.

7. Blueberry Almond Joy:

Ingredients: 1/2 cup blueberries, 1/4 cup almonds, 1 tablespoon honey, 1 cup almond milk, ice cubes.

Preparation: Blend until creamy.

Nutritional Value: Rich in antioxidants and protein.

Cooking Time: 5 minutes.

8. Peanut Butter Banana Oat Smoothie:

Ingredients: 1 banana, 2 tablespoons peanut butter, 1/4 cup oats, 1 cup milk (dairy or plant-based), ice cubes.

Preparation: Blend until oats are well incorporated.

Nutritional Value: Good source of fiber and protein.

Cooking Time: 5 minutes.

9. Avocado Berry Blast:

Ingredients: 1 ripe avocado, 1/2 cup mixed berries, 1 tablespoon honey, 1 cup coconut water, ice cubes.

Preparation: Blend until creamy.

Nutritional Value: High in healthy fats and antioxidants. Cooking Time: 5 minutes.

10. Cherry Almond Protein Smoothie:

Ingredients: 1/2 cup cherries (pitted), 1/4 cup almonds, 1 scoop protein powder, 1 cup almond milk, ice cubes.

Preparation: Blend until smooth.

Nutritional Value: Protein-packed with antioxidants.

Cooking Time: 5 minutes.

Bonus:15 Days Meal Planner

Menu List:

Breakfast

Lunch

Dinner

Important Meal:

shopping list:

● ....
● ....
● ....
● ....
● ....

To Do List
....
....
....
....

Notes And Tips

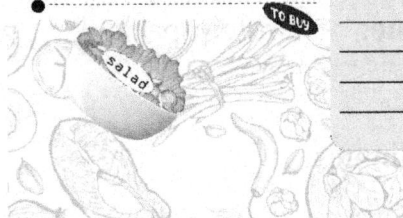

CHAPTER 6

Conclusion

In the closing pages of this weight gain cookbook tailored for seniors, we embark on a journey that transcends mere recipes—it's a celebration of vitality and well-being. Through thoughtful culinary guidance, we've redefined the narrative around senior nutrition, emphasizing the joy of nourishing both body and spirit. This book isn't just about adding pounds; it's a testament to the transformative power of wholesome meals, fostering resilience, and embracing the golden years with gusto.

As we bid farewell, remember that this isn't just a cookbook; it's a companion on your quest for a healthier, more vibrant life. Each recipe is a step toward reclaiming the pleasure of savoring meals and relishing the rich tapestry of flavors. May every dish bring fulfillment, reminding you that the journey to optimal health is a daily celebration—a symphony of tastes, textures, and memories that paint a portrait of a life well-lived.

Menu List:

Breakfast

Lunch

Dinner

Important Meal;

shopping list:

- ....
- ....
- ....
- ....
- ....

To Do List

....
....
....
....
....

Notes And Tips

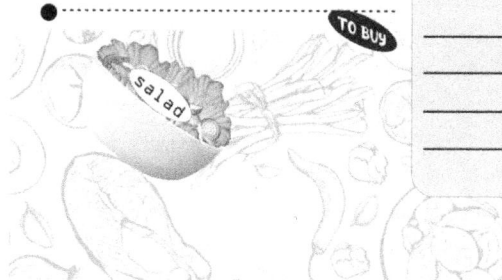

Menu List:

Breakfast

Lunch

Dinner

Important Meal;

shopping list:

To Do List
....
....
....
....
....

● ....

● ....

● ....

● ....

● ....

Notes And Tips

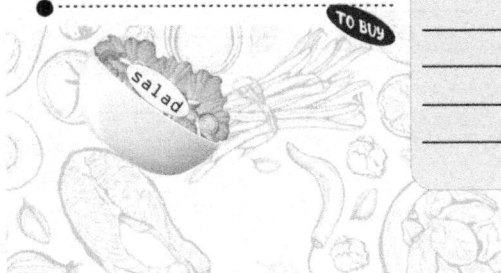

Menu List:

Breakfast

Lunch

Dinner

Important Meal;

shopping list:

To Do List

....

....

....

....

....

- ....

- ....

- ....

- ....

- ....

Notes And Tips To Do

TO BUY

salad

Menu List:

Breakfast

Important Meal;

Lunch

Dinner

shopping list:

To Do List
....
....
....
....
....

- ....
- ....
- ....
- ....
- ....

Notes And Tips TO DO

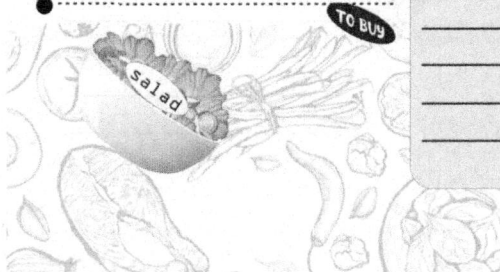

salad TO BUY

Menu List:

Breakfast

Lunch

Dinner

Important Meal:

shopping list:

To Do List

• ....

• ....

• ....

• ....

• ....

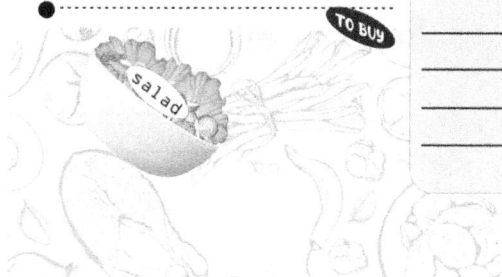

Notes And Tips   To Do

Menu List:

Breakfast

Lunch

Dinner

Important Meal;

shopping list:

- ....
- ....
- ....
- ....
- ....

To Do List
....
....
....
....
....

Notes And Tips

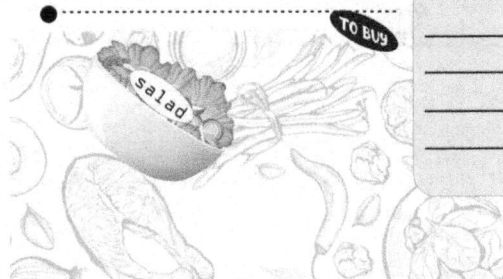

Menu List:

Breakfast

Lunch

Dinner

Important Meal;

shopping list:

- ....
- ....
- ....
- ....
- ....

TO BUY

salad

To Do List
....
....
....
....
....

Notes And Tips   TO DO

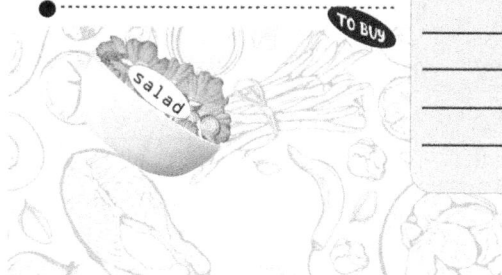

113

Menu List:

Breakfast

Lunch

Dinner

Important Meal;

shopping list:

- ....
- ....
- ....
- ....
- ....

To Do List

....
....
....
....
....

Notes And Tips

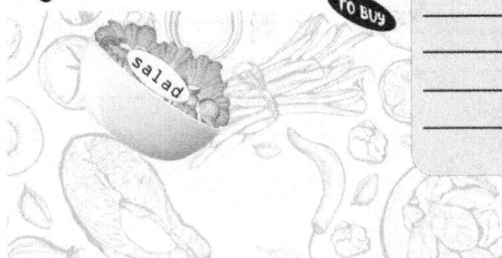

Menu List:

Breakfast

Lunch

Dinner

Important Meal;

shopping list:

- ....
- ....
- ....
- ....
- ....

TO BUY

salad

To Do List

....
....
....
....
....

Notes And Tips   TO DO

Menu List:

Breakfast

Lunch

Dinner

Important Meal;

shopping list:

To Do List

....
....
....
....
....

● ....

● ....

● ....

● ....

● ....

Notes And Tips

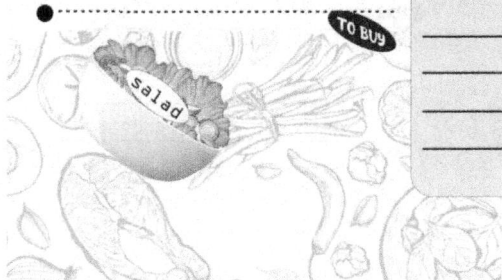

Menu List:

Breakfast

Lunch

Dinner

Important Meal;

shopping list:

- •⋯⋯⋯⋯⋯⋯⋯⋯⋯
- •⋯⋯⋯⋯⋯⋯⋯⋯⋯
- •⋯⋯⋯⋯⋯⋯⋯⋯⋯
- •⋯⋯⋯⋯⋯⋯⋯⋯⋯
- •⋯⋯⋯⋯⋯⋯⋯⋯⋯

To Do List

⋯⋯⋯⋯⋯⋯⋯⋯⋯⋯
⋯⋯⋯⋯⋯⋯⋯⋯⋯⋯
⋯⋯⋯⋯⋯⋯⋯⋯⋯⋯
⋯⋯⋯⋯⋯⋯⋯⋯⋯⋯
⋯⋯⋯⋯⋯⋯⋯⋯⋯⋯

Notes And Tips   To Do

TO BUY

salad

Menu List:

Breakfast

Lunch

Dinner

Important Meal;

shopping list:

- ....
- ....
- ....
- ....
- ....

To Do List

....
....
....
....
....

Notes And Tips

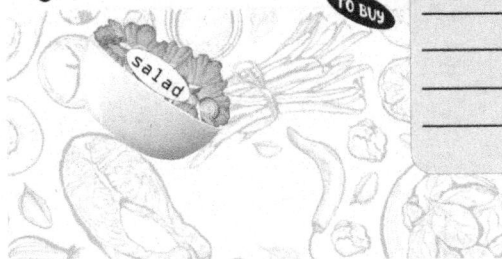

TO BUY

salad

Menu List:

Breakfast

Lunch

Dinner

Important Meal;

shopping list:

To Do List
····························
····························
····························
····························
····························

- ·····································
- ·····································
- ·····································
- ·····································
- ·····································

Notes And Tips

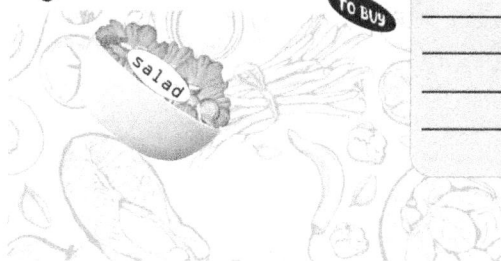

Menu List:

Breakfast

Lunch

Dinner

Important Meal:

shopping list:

● ....
● ....
● ....
● ....
● ....

To Do List
....
....
....
....
....

Notes And Tips

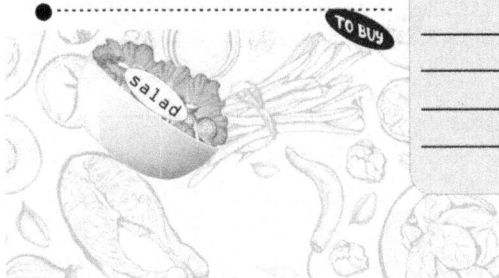

Menu List:

Breakfast

Lunch

Dinner

Important Meal;

shopping list:

- • ....
- • ....
- • ....
- • ....
- • ....

To Do List
....
....
....
....
....

Notes And Tips   To Do

Menu List:

Breakfast

Lunch

Dinner

Important Meal:

shopping list:

- ....
- ....
- ....
- ....
- ....

To Do List
....
....
....
....
....

Notes And Tips

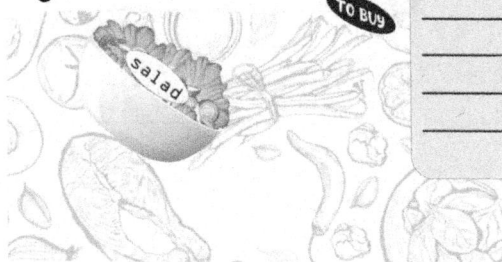

Made in the USA
Las Vegas, NV
08 December 2024